F. Isabel Campoy  Alma Flor Ada

Celebrate
Juneteenth
and Malik's Birthday

Illustrated by Nathalia Rivera
Translated by Lawrence Schimel

"Malik, look how many bags Mama's carrying!"

"Of course, Ayana! They must be things for my birthday party. I'm sure the round one is the basketball I asked for as a present!"

"Look, Malik: Grandma and Aunt Maya are sewing something nice."

"Of course, Ayana! It must be something for my birthday party. I'm sure it's the Superman costume I asked them for as a present!"

"Look, Malik! Grandpa has spent all day on the phone!"

"Of course, Ayana! I'm sure he's calling lots of people to invite them to my birthday party! I hope he invites cousins Martin and Michelle. We haven't seen them in a long time!"

"That's because they live far away, Malik."

"Grandpa, Grandpa!" Malik says, excitedly. "How many people are coming to my birthday party?"

"I don't have time now, kids. We're very busy organizing the Juneteenth celebration."

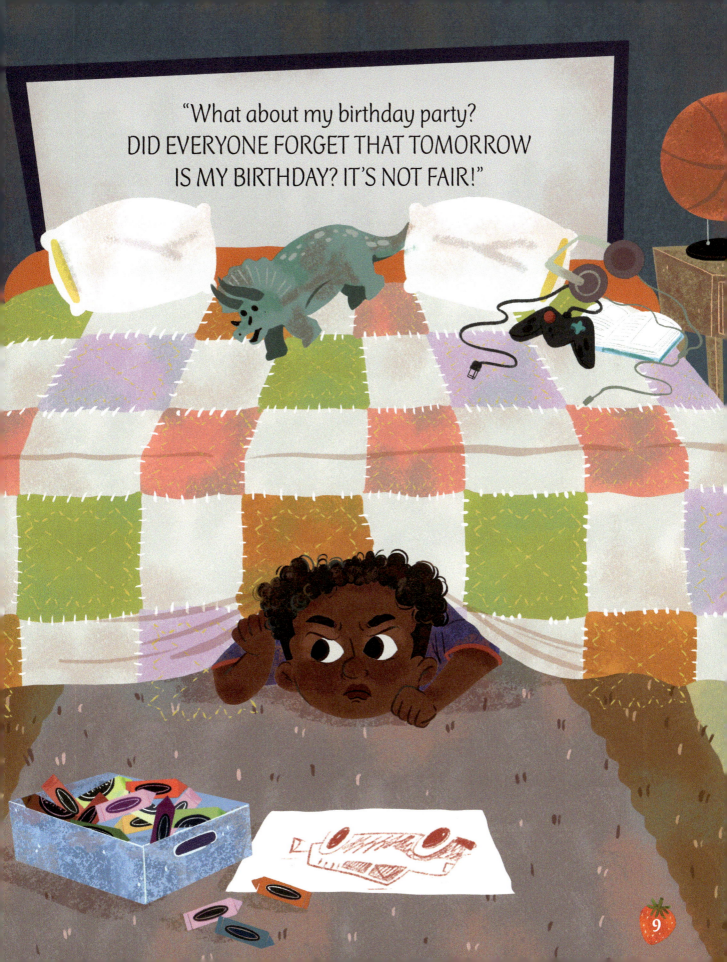

"Look who's here, Malik!" Ayana jumps for joy.

"We came to celebrate your birthday!" Michelle says.

"And something else that Papa says is called Juneteenth," Martin adds.

"Ayana and Malik, I have to say I'm sorry. I've been very stressed today. It's just that we want this great celebration to turn out perfectly."

"Are you talking about Juneteenth, Grandpa?" Malik asks.

"Yes, it is a celebration as important as your birthday, and they both fall on the same day!"

"Why is it important?" Michelle interrupts.

"On June 19, we celebrate the day when our ancestors learned that they were finally free."

"Free?" Martin is surprised.

"Yes, free from slavery. They no longer had to work for White slavers with no payment, or accept mistreatment. Freedom is something very valuable. That is why we will celebrate it in a big way, with the whole family!"

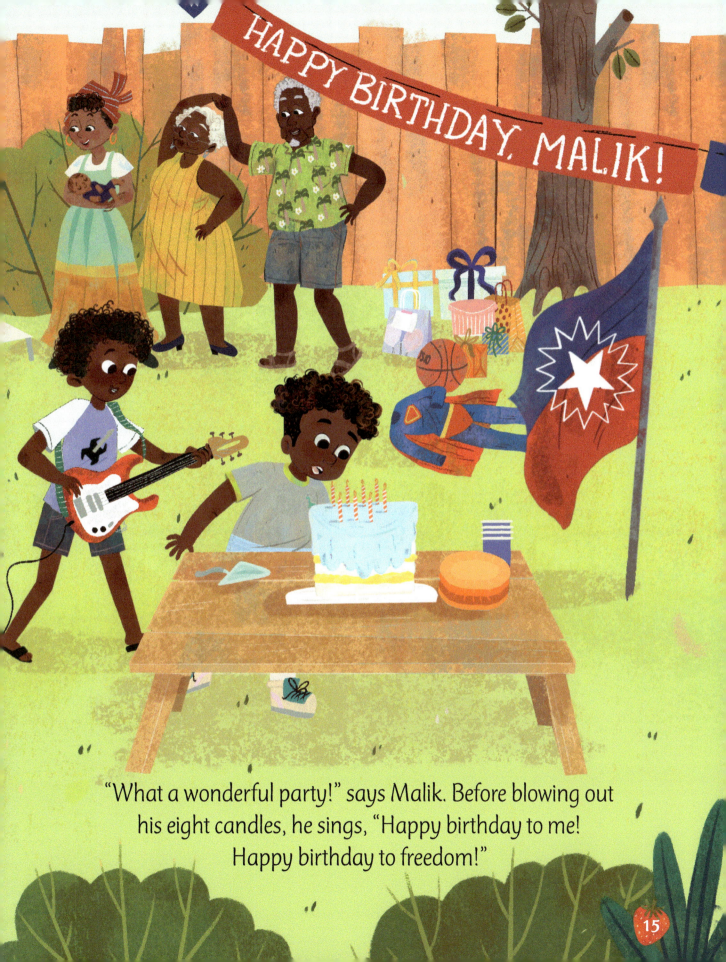

"What a wonderful party!" says Malik. Before blowing out his eight candles, he sings, "Happy birthday to me! Happy birthday to freedom!"

What Is Juneteenth?

Juneteenth is celebrated in honor of June 19, 1865, the date when enslaved Black Texans learned that they were finally free. The word Juneteenth is a combination of the words June and nineteenth.

On that day, a soldier, Major General Gordon Granger, read to the people of Galveston, Texas, a note from the government announcing that all enslaved people in the United States were free.

When they heard the word "free," the African Americans of Galveston began to leap, dance, and hug one another, shouting in jubilee. This meant they were no longer considered to be the property of their White enslavers. Freedom was a dream that many had believed would never come true. That is why this date is still celebrated with excitement to this day.

Slavery began in the 13 colonies in 1619. That year, the first of many ships arrived to Virginia full of Black people who were forced to come here from Africa to work the lands of White plantation owners. These people received no payment for their work and were often mistreated.

When the United States won the American Revolution in 1783, the people of the 13 colonies freed themselves from another country called Great Britain. However, the freedom of all Americans was not recognized. African Americans were not free until more than 80 years later.

SCENE ON A COTTON PLANTATION. GATHERING COTTON.

The USA During the Civil War

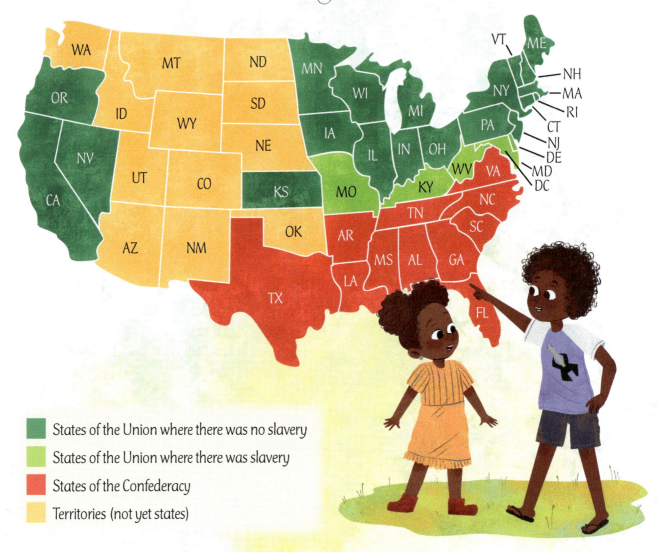

- States of the Union where there was no slavery
- States of the Union where there was slavery
- States of the Confederacy
- Territories (not yet states)

In 1861, slavery still existed in various states. Abraham Lincoln was elected president. Seven states in the South, where slavery was practiced, seceded, or separated, from the United States. They knew that Lincoln was opposed to slavery, so they formed their own country (called the Confederacy) to ensure that they could continue to enslave people.

The president told them that they could not do this. Then the Civil War broke out between the Confederacy and the states that remained in the Union. Four more states joined the Confederacy. On January 1, 1863, Lincoln signed the Emancipation Proclamation, a document that gave freedom to all enslaved people in the southern states.

In the end, the Union won the war and Lincoln granted freedom to all the Black people of the United States, no matter where they lived.

The African Americans of the state of Texas were the last to learn that slavery had been abolished in the United States. After the announcement read by General Granger on that June 19, this date soon became a day of celebration for all African Americans in Texas and the South.

O ver time, Juneteenth began to be celebrated in other states. And since 2021, it has been a federal holiday; that is to say, it is now a celebration for the entire country—a day of celebration for all Americans!

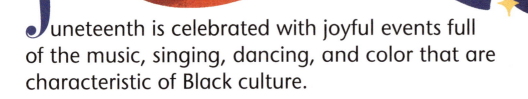

Juneteenth is celebrated with joyful events full of the music, singing, dancing, and color that are characteristic of Black culture.

Parades have also been very important since the first Juneteenth celebrations. Black soldiers who had fought in the Civil War led the parades, riding horses decorated with ribbons.

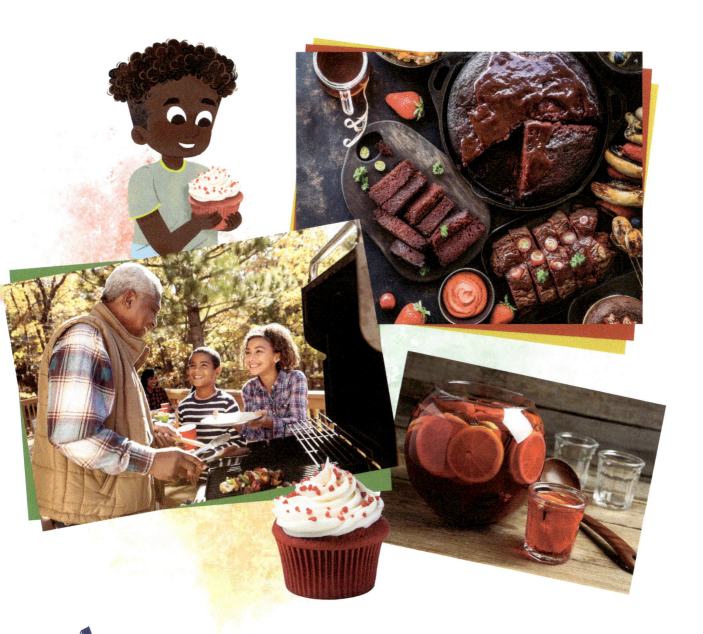

And of course it wouldn't be a celebration without delicious food—like cherries, strawberries, red velvet cake, watermelon, barbecue, and red punch. Did you notice that all those things are red? That is no coincidence; the color red represents the bravery and endurance, or ability to survive hardship, of enslaved people. Red also symbolizes the blood that was shed by Black people in their fight for freedom.

Other popular activities on Juneteenth are baseball games, fishing, and rodeos. People also wave the Juneteenth flag, which is red, white, and blue, the same colors as the American flag. At night, fireworks light up the sky.

You may think that the celebration of Juneteenth is very similar to the Fourth of July, or Independence Day. Well, that's because these two holidays are very similar. Both celebrate freedom. The main difference is that the Fourth of July celebrates Americans declaring themselves free from British power, while Juneteenth celebrates the day on which, at last, *all* Americans were free.

A multigenerational African American family.
© Stockbroker/123RF

Chalk writing on an old-fashioned blackboard explains the meaning of the word "Juneteenth."
© MarekPhotoDesign/Adobe Stock

A child takes part in a Juneteenth parade.
© Anaumenko/Adobe Stock (Generated by AI)

African Americans celebrating Juneteenth.
© Elena/Adobe Stock (Generated by AI)

Vintage engraved illustration (1880–1881) titled The Treaty, which shows a scene of the journey by ship carrying enslaved people from Africa to the Americas.
© PantherMediaSeller/Deposit Photos

A group of African Americans commemorate Juneteenth, dressing in clothes from the time when slavery was abolished in the United States.
© Lucas Comba/Adobe Stock (Generated by AI)

Close-up of Harriet Tubman Statue in the South End neighborhood of Boston, Massachusetts. Tubman fought for the freedom of enslaved people.
© Heidi Besen/Shutterstock

Old engraving that shows enslaved people working in a cotton plantation in the US, around 1860.
© Archivist/Adobe Stock

Historical depiction of President Abraham Lincoln signing the Emancipation Proclamation, the document that abolished slavery in the United States.
© Szalai/Adobe Stock (Generated by AI)

Penny showing the face of President Abraham Lincoln.
© Somchai Som/Shutterstock

Five-dollar bill showing the face of President Abraham Lincoln.
© Wedmoscow/Deposit Photos

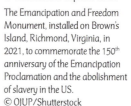
The Emancipation and Freedom Monument, installed on Brown's Island, Richmond, Virginia, in 2021, to commemorate the 150th anniversary of the Emancipation Proclamation and the abolishment of slavery in the US.
© OJUP/Shutterstock

A father and child taking part in the Second Annual Juneteenth Parade on Market Street, San Francisco, California.
© Sheilaf2002/Deposit Photos

People dressed in brightly colored clothing take part in a Juneteenth celebration.
© PrettyStock/Adobe Stock (Generated by AI)

A man and several children dance on a stage during a Juneteenth celebration in La Crosse, Wisconsin.
© Aaron of L.A. Photography/Shutterstock

A crowd is gathered on a sunny day to take part in the 13th Annual Juneteenth Celebration in Prospect Park, Brooklyn, New York.
© Wirestock Creators/Shutterstock

African American youth play drums in a Juneteenth celebration.
© DigitalArt Max/Adobe Stock (Generated by AI)

Police and firemen take part in the Second Annual Juneteenth Parade on Market Street, San Francisco, California.
© Sheilaf2002/Deposit Photos

Juneteenth parade in San Francisco, California.
© Sheila Fitzgerald/Shutterstock

African American girls wearing traditional African clothing ride on a float during a Juneteenth celebration.
© Pixardi/Adobe Stock (Generated by AI)

An African American family shares a barbecue to celebrate Juneteenth.
© Monkeybusiness/Deposit Photos

Traditional Juneteenth food, such as barbecued meats, red velvet cake, and strawberries.
© Kateryna/Adobe Stock (Generated by AI)

Red velvet cake, one of the traditional desserts of Juneteenth celebrations.
© Rawpixel (Generated by AI)

Red punch, one of the traditional beverages of Juneteenth celebrations.
© NewAfrica/Deposit Photos

The Juneteenth flag waving beside the American flag.
© Rarrarorro/Deposit Photos

A group of children watching fireworks, one of the ways that Juneteenth is celebrated.
© Wavebreakmediamicro/123RF

A group of Americans of different ethnic backgrounds and ages come together to celebrate Juneteenth.
© Rawpixel

Celebrate and Grow

Throughout history, and in all parts of the world, people get together to celebrate historic anniversaries, commemorate an important person's life, or to ring in a special period of the year. Common to all these celebrations is the acknowledgment that life is a marvelous gift, and that getting together with family and friends makes us happy.

In a multicultural society, like that found in the United States, the fact that so many diverse groups live so closely together invites us to know our own culture better, and to discover the cultures of others. Anyone who explores their own culture recognizes their own identity in the mirror and affirms their sense of belonging to a group. By learning about different cultures, we can observe life as it appears through the windows of those cultures.

This series offers children the opportunity to get close to the rich cultural landscape of our communities.

Juneteenth

There are moments in history that must be remembered because they mark a very important change in the society that celebrates them. Juneteenth marked the end of an injustice that should never have occurred. After four years of Civil War between the North and the South of the United States, on June 19, 1865, General Granger reached Galveston, Texas with the happy news that the African American population had been granted freedom and now could never again be enslaved.

For more than a century and a half, that day has been a happy occasion on which African American families and communities come together so that their dignity and their freedom are not forgotten. In 2021, Juneteenth was declared a federal holiday for all the people of the United States, a country with "freedom and justice for all," as the Pledge of Allegiance of our nation states. Music, good food, and dancing enliven the celebration of this great date.

F. Isabel Campoy & Alma Flor Ada

For Ziana, including me in her joy. Always with love.
FIC

For my great granddaughter Ziana, celebrating her heritage and freedom. With immense love.
AFA

© 2025, Vista Higher Learning, Inc.
500 Boylston Street, 10th Floor
Boston, MA 02116-3736
www.vistahigherlearning.com
www.loqueleo.com/us

Text copyright: © 2025, F. Isabel Campoy and Alma Flor Ada

Creative Director: José A. Blanco
Executive Vice-president and General Manager, K–12: Vincent Grosso
Executive Editor: Julie McCool
Editorial: Salwa Lacayo, Isabel C. Mendoza
Design: Radoslav Mateev, Gabriel Noreña, Verónica Suescún, Andrés Vanegas, Manuela Zapata
Project Management: Karys Acosta, Tiffany Kayes
Rights: Jorgensen Fernandez, Annie Pickert Fuller, Kristine Janssens
Production: Thomas Casallas, Oscar Díez, Sebastián Díez, Andrés Escobar, Adriana Jaramillo, Daniel Lopera, Daniela Peláez
Illustrator: Nathalia Rivera
Translator: Lawrence Schimel

Celebrate Juneteenth and Malik's Birthday
ISBN: 978-1-66993-520-9

A New Sunrise / Un nuevo amanecer © F. Isabel Campoy (artwork & photo, page 3)

All rights reserved. No part of this book may be reproduced or transmitted in any form or by any means, electronic or mechanical, including photocopying, recording or by any information storage and retrieval system, without permission in writing from the publisher.

Printed in the United States of America

1 2 3 4 5 6 7 8 9 GP 30 29 28 27 26 25